In memory of S. Balbir Singh Sodhi, a Sikh and the first person
innocently killed in the aftermath of 9-11-01 because he wore a turban.
We shall never forget him.

A portion of the proceeds from the sale of this book will be donated to the children of
S. Balbir Singh Sodhi for their future education.

© 2004 LEADERSHIP BY TURBAN™
ALL RIGHTS RESERVED

Published by :

Hemkunt Publishers Private Limited
A-78, Naraina Industrial Area, Phase I,
New Delhi - 110 028 (India)
Tel.   : 2579-2083, 2579-0032, 2579-5079
Fax   : 91-11-2611-3705
E-mail   : hemkunt@ndf.vsnl.net.in
Website   : www.hemkuntpublishers.com

ISBN : 81-7010-333-9

Printed and bound in India.

LEADERSHIP BY TURBAN™

AN AMERICAN STORY

Editor: Mike Scholtz

Book Designer: Dalbir Singh

Photographer: Amit Sharma

Special thanks to my family for their love, to my friends for their loyalty, and God for inspiration and courage to complete this project.

TABLE OF CONTENTS

Page

1.	an american story	7
2.	why the turban	8
3.	frequently asked questions	9
4.	leadership	14
5.	understand your mission	17
6.	to learn is to grow	22
7.	play life's little games	30
8.	in god we trust	33

Page

9. the unwritten rules   38

10. live 24 hours a day   44

11. where you come from   56

12. there is no greater wealth   62

13. no limits   70

14. it's all up to you   78

15. branding by turban   84

16. turbans for everyone   86

IF JUST ONE PERSON GAINS
A PEARL OF KNOWLEDGE FROM THIS BOOK
THEN I HAVE ACCOMPLISHED
WHAT I HOPED TO ACHIEVE BY WRITING IT.

Leadership by Turban is a true American story about a young man seeking to balance his religious identity in today's America. Ravi Singh writes vividly about his daily struggles wearing a turban, highlighting principles of leadership we can all use in our daily lives.

Ravi Singh was born and raised in Illinois. In 1990, he graduated from Marmion Military Academy, making history by becoming the first US cadet ever to graduate from a military academy with a turban. He's been an aide to the lieutenant governor & state treasurer of Illinois, a student body president, an NCAA Division I golf captain, a candidate for public office, a community activist, involved in two presidential campaigns, an international lecturer, and business entrepreneur. His story challenges our pre-conceptions about life in the US and makes us rethink what it means to be an American.

NOBODY HAS ALL THE ANSWERS BECAUSE NOBODY KNOWS ALL THE QUESTIONS.

SOCIETY SEES US ONE WAY
WE NEED TO PRESENT OURSELVES ANOTHER WAY
LEADERSHIP IS THE ANSWER

I am an American. And I wear a turban. A lot of people think that's an odd combination. They wonder how I balance these two influences on my life. And whether I find my turban a poor fit in modern America. I have to admit, I've wondered, too. For years, I searched for answers in the words of great authors, scholars, philosophers and CEOs. But, as it turned out, the answer was with me all along. I found them in myself. In my life. In my experiences. From academics to politics to business and religion, these experiences have made me proud to be who I am. They've made me proud to be an American. And they've made me proud to wear my turban.

I believe that truth is the most valuable gift you can share with other people. And that's why I'm sharing my truths. These are the stories of my life that shaped my values and principles. Through trial and error, I had to learn the hard way how to stand up for myself. Wearing a turban hasn't always been easy, but it's taught me some interesting lessons about being a leader. I hope people can learn something from my experiences. Not just about guys who wear turbans, but about leadership. Because the future is coming and for our children's sake we should be better prepared to lead it.

Chapter 2
why the turban

When I was born, my parents wrapped my head with a soft hand-knitted cotton cloth. Little did I know it then, but I would wear a turban for the rest of my life. I remember going to school and hearing other children make jokes about me. I had to befriend the bus driver for protection from the abuse I received. Young Sikh boys are required to wear a pre-turban over their head until they get facial hair. My knee length hair was tied in a braided bun and wrapped under a piece of cloth with four strings. It wasn't something people saw very often amongst the cornfields of Illinois. Children called me names. Some told me I looked like a girl.

In the fifth grade, I decided to abandon the pre-turban and wear a real turban. It wasn't so much to feel grown-up as it was to stop the name-calling. My father yelled and screamed that I was not ready. Didn't he understand that having a bun on my head was difficult to explain to the other children? Didn't he know that wearing a blue pre-turban made me look like a cartoon Smurf? Apparently not. Growing up with a different religion isn't easy for anyone.

And wearing a turban seemed particularly difficult to me at the time. But through every episode of my life, my turban has been there, as a symbol of my religion, leading the way.

CAMEL JOCKEY AND BASEBALLHEAD WERE COMMONLY HEARD AROUND THE JUNGLE GYM. GROWING UP, I HAD MORE FIGHTS DEFENDING MY TURBAN THAN I CARE TO REMEMBER. IN THE BEGINNING, I WAS GIVEN MY TURBAN. BUT IN THE END, I CHOSE TO DEFEND IT.

Originally, I wore
the turban for
my religion.
Then for my family.
Now I wear it for
myself.

MY HAIR STATS	
The hair can never be cut	
Q1	How long is your hair?
A1	*It's about 4½ feet long and really curly.*
Q2	Can you ever shave or trim your beard?
A2	*No, but I can compress it with styling gel.*
Q3	How long does it take to wash it?
A3	*About 30 minutes with a lot of shampoo & conditioner*
Q4	Do you ever wear it down?
A4	*Of course - around the house, but never in public.*

– I am a member of the Sikh religion, founded in northern India in 1469. Sikhs believe in one universal God. And that the truth is the highest form of salvation.

– I was born and raised in the United States. One of the articles of faith I am required to wear is a turban. That is not an easy thing to do in a country where Sikhs are a visible minority. But I've overcome the challenge and worn my turban despite all the criticism and racism I faced growing up.

– The turban was first given as a gift to my religion, along with five other symbols, by the tenth teacher of Sikhism, Guru Gobind Singh. In 1699, Guru Gobind Singh asked Sikhs to accept these symbols as a teacher gives a gift to his students. Those who wear turbans take on the daily challenge of representing the Sikh faith.

MY TURBAN STATS

The turban is tied daily

Q1 How long is your turban?

A1 It's usually about 18 feet long.

Q2 What is it made out of?

A2 Mine is made of voil, a fine cotton.

Q3 How long does it take to tie it?

A3 5 minutes on a good day. Otherwise, it can take 20 minutes.

Q4 Do you sleep with it?

A4 Everyone always asks me that question. The answer is "NO".

– The turban is a religious article about 6 yards long made out of cotton.

– The turban is tied daily.

– I wear my turban in public because Sikhs are not allowed to cut their hair. My knee-length hair symbolizes my strength, like the story of Samson in the Old Testament. It represents my faith, reminding me that the Creator is God to all.

– In British-occupied India, Sikhs were known for their chivalry. Their turbans symbolized their obligation to society to be righteous and uphold justice at all time. I am committed to that same code, defending the weak and helping the poor, regardless of race, creed, religion or sex.

TERMINOLOGY

Turbanology

T1	*Fifty*	=	The triangle under the turban
T2	*Dis-tar*	=	The pre-turban
T3	*Pony*	=	How you fold the turban
T4	*Laar*	=	Each fold of the turban

Symbols of Faith

T5	*Kesh*	=	Uncut hair
T6	*Kacha*	=	Boxer shorts
T7	*Kanga*	=	Comb
T8	*Kara*	=	Stainless steel bracelet
T9	*Kirpan*	=	Small sword

– The turban identifies the 26 million Sikhs around the world, making it the 5th largest religion in the world. It allows them to be singled out in a crowd. But at the same time, obligates them to meet the honorable code of doing good at all time.

– My turban and my uncut hair define me, my moral values and my commitment to God and country. I am who I am because of my turban. Wearing it, I have overcome tremendous odds and accomplished great things.

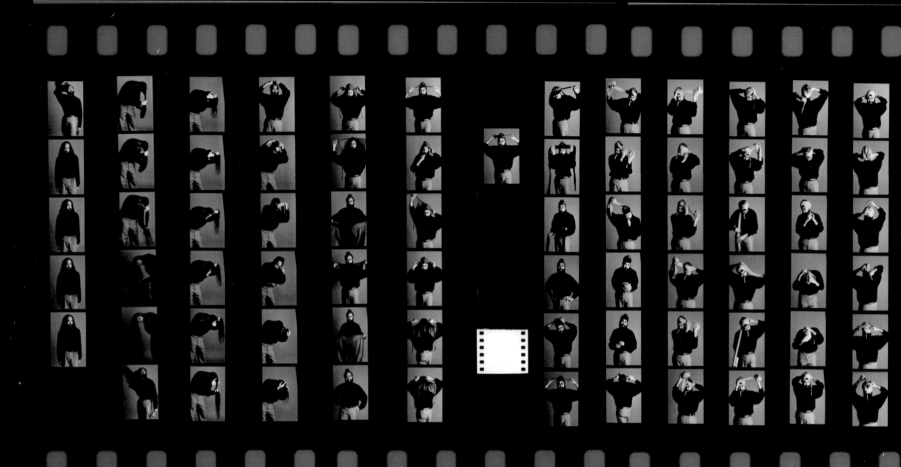

In spite of obstacles and dangers and pressures, a man does what he must - in spite of personal consequences, and that is the basis of all human morality.

– JOHN F KENNEDY

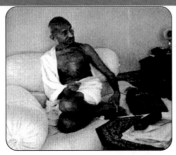

I could not be leading a religious life unless I identified myself with the whole of mankind, and that I could not unless I took part in politics.

– M. K. GANDHI

I claim not to have controlled events, but confess plainly that events have controlled me.

– ABRAHAM LINCOLN

Never regard study as a duty but an enviable opportunity to learn.

– ALBERT EINSTEIN

EVERY DAY WE ALL DO SOMETHING THAT MAKES US A LEADER.

What is leadership? It's been defined in many different ways. By many different people. John F. Kennedy illustrated it through his youthful charisma. M. K. Gandhi showed us the possibilities of passive resistance in freeing a nation. Abraham Lincoln demonstrated strength in keeping a nation united by principles and values. And Albert Einstein showed us that one individual's mind can be used as a tool to solve the mysteries of the universe.

Each of these leaders added an element to our society's elusive, constantly-evolving definition of leadership. But, in the end, I don't believe leadership is something we can really define for other people. We can only attempt to illustrate it. That's what I hope to accomplish with this book. Because leadership is something that can be learned. If each of us makes the effort, we can change our life and the lives of others.

TO TRULY LEAD MEANS PUTTING ASIDE YOUR OWN DESIRES AND AMBITIONS TO BETTER YOUR COUNTRY, YOUR RELIGION, YOUR COMMUNITY, YOUR BUSINESS AND YOUR FAMILY, INSPIRING THEM TO BECOME MORE THAN THEY WOULD HAVE EVER IMAGINED.

LEARN TO FOLLOW OTHERS AND OTHERS WILL EVENTUALLY FOLLOW YOU.

EXCELLENT LEADERS ARE MADE AS WELL AS BORN. TO BE THE BEST LEARN THE ESSENTIAL SKILLS OF LEADERSHIP THROUGH TRAINING AND EXPERIENCE.

LEARN TO LEAD YOURSELF -

PHYSICALLY, INTELLECTUALLY, EMOTIONALLY, AND SPIRITUALLY

BEFORE YOU DECIDE TO LEAD OTHERS.

GOD, COUNTRY, DUTY AND HONOR BECAME PART OF MY LIFE.

PHOTO: MARMION MILITARY ACADEMY AURORA, ILLINOIS BEACON STAFF PHOTOGRAPHER.

When I was 14 years old, I was sent to Catholic military academy. It was a place full of contradictions. On the one hand, our theology class taught us to love our neighbor. On the other, we learned how to shoot a rifle. But the contradiction of a cadet who happened to wear a turban was something the academy had never before seen. It was almost too great to overcome.

From my first day at Marmion Military Academy, I had doubts about whether or not I could make it. I loved my academy. I loved my country. But I also loved my turban. Shortly after I arrived, the headmaster called me into his office for a serious talk. He told me that the military had decided my turban was not compliant with the safety and health regulations of the Junior Reserve Officers Training Corps (JROTC). My parents were devastated. They could not understand why my headmaster would make such an example of an American-born boy like me. But I was actually happy. Who wanted to go to an all boy school at the age of 14, anway? It was not until I spoke to my grandfather that I realized how important it was for me to stay. He told me, "If you don't fight this, then no one else will. You need to set the example, since you are the first."

PHOTO: GRADUATION MARMION MILITARY ACADEMY.

Sikhs believe they have an obligation to be righteous and just. That's why Sikhs, honored for their valor, by so many countries, have such a strong tradition in the Indian Military. True, the pen is mightier than the sword. But our "saint and soldier" philosophy calls on us to raise our swords to defend our rights or the rights of others. And one of the rights we hold most dear is freedom of speech. We may not agree with what someone has said, but we will fight to the death for their right to say it.

I DIDN'T WANT TO BE THE FIRST
ONE WITH A TURBAN IN THE
MILITARY ACADEMY. BUT I DIDN'T WANT TO BE
THE LAST ONE EITHER.

Along with my obligations to righteousness and justice, my education at the military academy taught me the importance of honor, duty, loyalty and tradition. I soon came to realize that the only way to live up to all these values was by embracing my turban.

So my mother asked for help from our representatives in Congress, Dennis Hastert and John Porter. On my behalf, they introduced legislation that would allow me to graduate with my turban. Although President Ronald Reagan signed it into law, the Armed Service Committee overturned it. Even today, Sikhs are still not allowed to wear their turbans in active duty.

Thanks to special waiver from Secretary of Defense Dick Cheney, I graduated with full military honours as a 2nd Lieutenant. I didn't realize it at the time, but I had been making history every day at Marmion Military Academy simply by being there. I was the first cadet ever to graduate from an American military academy wearing a turban.

My grandfather was right. It was a **battle** that had to be fought.

Choosing a college is one of the biggest decisions anyone will ever make at the age of 18. Where will we study? After military academy, I thought that almost anything would be better than an all boys Catholic School. My parents came from the old country, where people judged you not on which college you went to, but on which Ivy League school you attended.

EDUCATION IS THE WEAPON
YOU USE TO FIGHT AGAINST THE ODDS IN
ACHIEVING YOUR TRUE DESTINY

If you weren't in the Ivy League, your parents were to blame. (Indian society-you gotta love it.) Out of respect for my mother and father, I applied to Brown University. And though I considered West Point, I knew it would be out of the question. Valparaiso University - in Indiana, the land of Hoosiers - offered me a golf scholarship as well as a multi-cultural scholarship, so I decided to go there. And for my parents sake, I just thank God, Valparaiso was ranked in the top 5 private schools in the Midwest.

PHOTO: STUDENT BODY PRESIDENT @ VALPARAISO UNIVERSITY

STUDENTS LEADERSHIP ISN'T A POPULARITY CONTEST
IT'S A **COMMUNICATION CONTEST.**

Around campus, building a reputation is easy to do when you're the only guy with a turban. But, a good reputation is a little more difficult to come by. So, I hung around at all the key events and dressed in the latest clothes—co-ordinating them, of course, with my turban. But no matter how hard you try, the world often has a way of overshadowing the efforts of the individual. In 1991, Sadaam Hussein invaded Kuwait. Within months America was fighting the Persian Gulf War. Instantly, people's perceptions about me changed. In the eyes of many, the front page of the newspaper defined me more than anything I said or did. Students and locals alike harassed me and called me names. I received phone calls in the middle of the night and death threats on my answering machine. Sadly, this was nothing new. In 1979, I was called Khomeini by people angry about the Iran hostage crisis. During the 80's, after the Marine barracks were bombed in Beirut, people called me a Palestinian terrorist. Even worse, Indian Prime Minister Indira Gandhi attacked the Sikh Vatican in Amritsar in 1984 and labeled Sikhs the country's number one militant group and terrorist faction. And now this - people calling me an Iraqi. Does it every stop? It was a tough lesson to have to learn once again. And an odd welcome to my new school.

Popularity can only take you so far. You still must stand for something.

THE STUDENTS HAD TO
LOOK BEYOND MY TURBAN
AND APPRECIATE WHAT I COULD DO AS STUDENT BODY PRESIDENT
RATHER THAN WHAT I LOOKED LIKE.

Things got better. But not without some difficulty. When I first ran for student body president at Valparaiso University, people told me there was no way a guy with a turban could win. 96% of the student body was caucasian. And Valparaiso University was the largest Lutheran college in the United States. So I tried to get all the cool kids to like me by outspending my opponents. I thought it was a sure thing. But I was wrong. Student leadership isn't popularity contest. It's about being sincere. It's about ideas and creativity and selling yourself. Only then can you win. The second time I ran, the cool kids still liked me. But I also had something to say.

"i" plan

innovate
investigate
initiate
implement

I had a plan of action I called the "I" plan. Innovate. Investigate. Initiate, Implement. I promised to be innovative when it came to solving problems. I would investigate every concern. I would initiate plans. I thought would work. And I would implement them untill I saw results. Thanks to the "I" plan - along with my skills, my education and, of course, a little popularity. I became the first turban-wearing student body president of Valparaiso University.

"WHAT YOU DO IN SCHOOL DETERMINES WHAT YOU DO IN LIFE. SO BE SMART. STUDY WHAT YOU LIKE BUT MAKE SURE YOU CAN LIVE OFF THE KNOWLEDGE YOU ATTAIN. BY FEEDING YOUR BRAIN YOU PHYSICALLY FEED YOURSELF FOR A LIFETIME."

When I told my parents about the election, they responded with one word. "Why?" They didn't understand why I wanted to do it. Like all good Indian parents they wanted me to become a doctor or an engineer. I preferred political science, but I didn't want to be considered an unworthy son. As first-generation immigrants, my parents believed their children should always do as they're told - never challenging, never showing their true feelings.

So I studied pre-med, with minors in chemistry and biology. After a few years, my parents slowly began to appreciate the things I wanted out of life. They came to understand my dreams and accept them. This didn't happen overnight - it came from mutual respect and from not hiding the truth. After three years as a pre-med student, my parents finally accepted that it wasn't my strongest subject. Meanwhile, I completed another degree in political science. It was a riskier path, but one that I found much more rewarding.

I believe you should follow your heart, because you have to live with yourself. Today, I still study constantly. I study books, I study magazines, I study people. To me, education is about more than passing exams and scoring grades. It's about learning for the rest of your life. But society keeps asking for our grades to figure out where we fit in. People often ask me about my degree: "What did you study? Where did you study?" But I don't think that's really important. What matters to me is where, when and how we apply our knowledge. Without an accurate understanding of the how the world works, it's impossible to lead.

If you don't know it, have someone teach it to you, if there is no one to teach you, teach YOURSELF!

I believe every leader should be a student of life. Just as every Sikh should be. In fact, the literal meaning of the word "Sikh" in Sanskrit means a "student." Every day, we're encouraged to learn just a little bit more. We'll never learn all the answers, but to stop trying would be to destroy one self.

Chapter 7
play life's little games

Some say golf is the most exciting sport you can learn. Others say it's the most boring. But no matter what you think about the game, competition can teach us invaluable skills about leadership.

I learned how to play golf when I was 12. My mother thought it would be a great way to spend time with my father. Because of their culture, my parents tended to be more reserved. Golf helped open the doors of communication with my traditional father. It was an ingenious plan on my mother's part, because my father and I could only talk about school for so long. By the second hole, we would run out of small talk and started to open up to each other. I found the same thing to be true later in life, when golf opened doors to me in politics and business, helping me to network and build relationships with others.

SINGH PINGH
GOLF CLASSIC

TIGER SHOWED US ALL THAT BEING DIFFERENT DIDN'T MATTER. HOW YOU PLAYED THE GAME DID. SO PLAY TO WIN.

My early instruction in golf paid off ten-fold. I completed in high school and later in college. At Valparaiso University, I was the first Indian to Captain an NCAA Division I golf team. But things didn't always go smoothly. On one memorable occasion, my team was not allowed to compete in a tournament held at a private club. For some reason, the members of the club refused to to let us play. As we were leaving, our coach told us not to worry about it. He said it had something to do with a fight he'd had with the organizers. Only later did he admit the truth - it was because of my turban. "It was the most racist and ridiculous thing I had ever heard," he complained to us. We were all shocked.

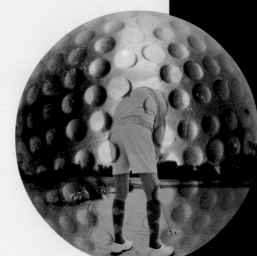

GOLF IS A GAME OF MISTAKES, THE QUESTION IS NOT MAKING THEM AGAIN, AGAIN AND AGAIN.

Can this really happen in America today? It's hard to believe, but many private clubs still discriminate against women, African Americans, and members of the Jewish faith. Four years later, I found myself facing a similar situation. At a corporate golf outing, the members tried to intimidate me right out of the club. If I had not been a low handicap player whose participation was so crucial to our tream's scramble, I might not have been allowed to play. It made me realize that with a turban, you have got to be the best in order to make people break the rules. And these are the rules that need to be broken. You can try to play a sport solely for the sport of it. But too often, we find ourselves playing life's little games, as well. Even today, I work hard to keep my game in the single digit handicaps, just so I can play golf at those special outings.

Golf opened other doors for me as well, doors that might otherwise have been closed. I was once asked to help raise money for charity at a golf outing. On a small par 3 hole, the objective was to get a lower score than me. Of, course there was a trick, I would be blindfolded while the other players would not. Who would have guessed that the relationships I built at that golf outing have lasted me a lifetime? Networking is a crucial skill. The ability to build sincere relationships can help us in everything we do.

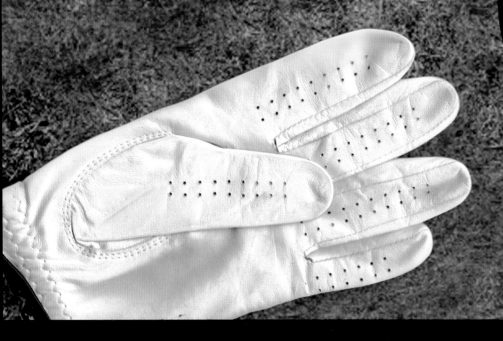

In golf, I was taught to swing and be patient. Golf is a game of consistency. It's the same swing, repeated over and over again. Once we get it right, we frame it in our minds and repeat it again and again. It is the same with leadership. Once we get the hang of something, we repeat it again and again. Granted, it takes a lot of practice to get it the way we want it. But in leadership, just as in golf, we have to slow down and take it one swing at a time.

When the time came for me to attend high school, my parents decided I needed to have a better understanding of Christianity. Only by studying one of the most popular religions in the world, would I come to better understand my own. Four years of Catholic education under the watchful eye of Benedictine monks - as well as four years at a Lutheran college - exposed me to the message of Christ and the story of the Bible. But at the same time, it gave me a perspective on my own faith. I no longer accepted things blindly. I began to question. I began to study. I began to realize the true meaning of being. That's how I came to accept my identity.

I AM NOT RELIGIOUS
I JUST BELIEVE

PHOTO: HOLINESS DALAI LAMA NOBEL PEACE PRIZE WINNER.

This idea of studying and comparing different faiths certainly isn't new. At the 1893 World Fair in Chicago, religious leaders from around the globe came together for the first time to do just that. And one hundred years later, the 1993 Parliament of World Religions united these diverse faiths again in Chicago, Illinois. Along with 8,000 others, I attended this event to explore the role of religion and spirituality in the modern world. There, I was the youngest person to sign "Towards a Global Ethic: An Initial Declaration." It was a historic statement of the ethical common ground shared by the world's religious traditions. Other signers included such leaders as the Dalai Lama, the Buddhist leader and Nobel Peace Prize winner, Cardinal Bernadine, the head of the Chicago Catholic Church, and Minister Louis Farrakhan, the head of the Nation of Islam.

While attending the Parliament of World Religions, I was chosen to chair the Next Generation Plenary Sessions. After months of preparations and interfaith dialogue, I organized an event that hosted more than 4,000 people at the historic Palmer House Hotel in Chicago. Addressing the audience, I implored them to put aside the label and "isms" that divide us. I said, "if we are one, we should act as one and unite under the common principles of unity, love and respect."

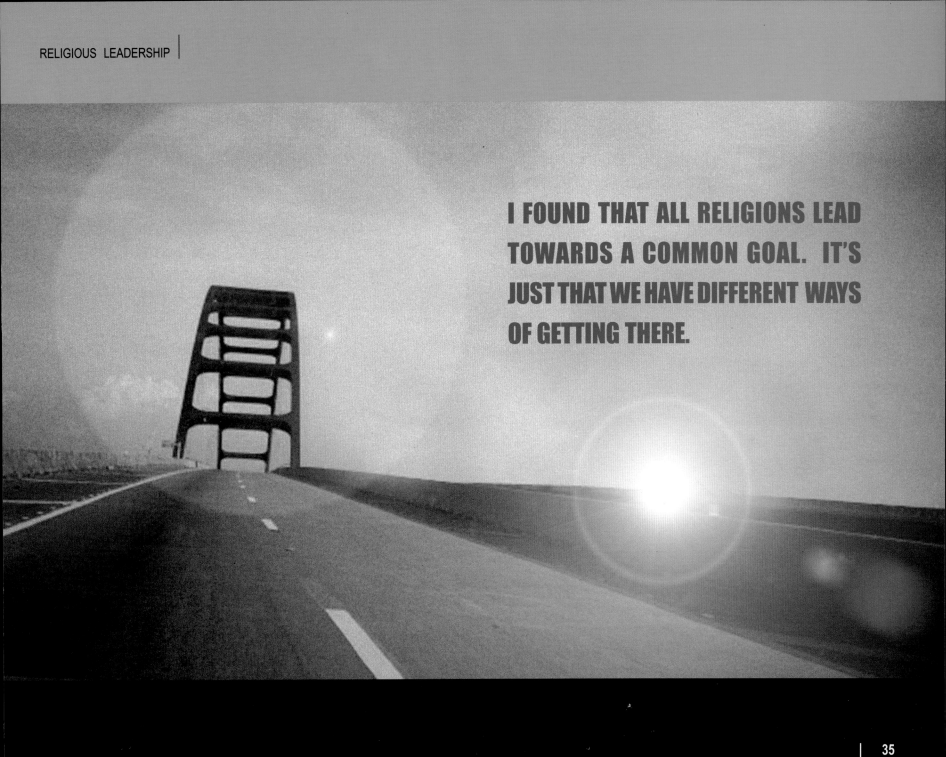

I FOUND THAT ALL RELIGIONS LEAD TOWARDS A COMMON GOAL. IT'S JUST THAT WE HAVE DIFFERENT WAYS OF GETTING THERE.

MAYA (or material wealth) DOES NOT LEAVE WITH YOU WHEN YOU DEPART FROM THIS WORLD.

Because I wear a turban, many people ask me, "Are you super-religious?" and "Do you meditate a lot?" I find these questions flattering, but stereotypical. Historically, the turban has held special significance for many different faiths, from the three kings of Judaism to the Asian kings who wore them as crowns to the many members of the Muslim faith who wear them as part of their cultural dress.

I wear my turban as a religious article of my faith, to cover uncut hair. But I don't think that makes me "super-religious." Grante I do meditate. But I think we all do, subconsciously at least. T larger question is how does each of us meditate? When we fi start driving we're focussed on getting from point A to point But after a while, we can listen to the radio or even carry on conversation while we are behind the wheel. This is a form subconscious meditation better known as multi-tasking, somethi we can all train our brains to do.

IT IS THE WEALTH FOUND IN RELATIONSHIPS WITH OTHERS THAT DOES.

Religious leadership begins with feeding the soul. We feed our bodies every day of our lives, but we must not forget our soul. We live in a materialistic world where people think they need to gather and collect things. Sometimes, I even find myself wishing for a designer Christian Dior turban. The Sikh word for material wealth is *"maya."*

I was taught to meditate on God's name - *Waheguru* - with every breath I take. It's a challenge, to say the least, but it is possible. I believe that wearing my turban helps me to focus on this task. It helps me to understand these concepts more keenly and to perform them in my daily life.

Maya may help us to live more comfortably, but using it to define our success can only be a never-ending battle. Instead, we must feed our soul by doing good. Only by doing good will other good people gravitate towards us.

When it comes to politics, I'm an Asian-American. The political establishment has little use for an Indian, a Sikh or a Punjabi. But once I defined myself as an Asian-American, I could lump myself in with Chinese, Koreans, Filipinos, Vietnamese, Japanese, Burmese, Pakistanis and Indians. Altogether, it's a pretty big constituency. And I was considered an asset as long as I was a part of it. This label helped me get my first job. And it helped me gain access to the "good ol boys" network in Illinois politics.

Politics always comes down to just two things. Money and votes. If you can't provide one or the other, people don't pay much attention to you. I may not call myself an Asian-American in any other setting, but politics is a game of perceptions. I had to find my niche and stick with it. So, when the lieutenant governor's office asked me to handle the Internet, my mother gave me the best advice. "Make friends with the 'gora munhda'" she said. "The white boy who knows how to do it." My "gora" was Todd Burke, who taught me everything there was to know about the Internet.

When I started in politics, my first job was to push mail from one building to another at the state capitol. Considering that I had a master's degree, it wasn't very satisfying. But I had to prove my worth in order to succeed. Few people wanted to see me succeed. Actually, few people want to see anyone succeed. I had to choose my friends wisely. And trust my instincts. That's what political leadership is about. Learning to trust our instincts. That's why we have to surround ourselves with positive people who share our agenda. Otherwise, we'll stay in the mail room with our master's degree for the rest of our career.

I KNEW WHERE I WANTED TO BE
BUT I FOUND OUT NO MATTER WHAT OR WHO YOU ARE.
YOU HAVE TO WORK YOUR WAY UP FROM THE BOTTOM.

PHOTO: ILLINOIS LT. GOVERNOR BOB KUSTRA

I NEVER KNEW WHAT A PROMISE REALLY MEANT, UNTIL I WORKED IN GOVERNMENT.

I met Judy Baar Topinka, the Illinois State Treasurer, at the State Fair in 1995. I was teaching a farmer how to use the Internet. She took one look at me and said, "We could use you in community relations in Chicago." By 1996, I was heading her Community Relations Department, working with community leaders and speaking on her behalf at various functions. A large part of being useful in public service is getting noticed. And nothing is more noticeable than a guy with a turban. Soon, everybody knew me as the liaison to the State Treasurer's office.

EVERY POLITICIAN I WORKED FOR HAD A DIFFERENT STYLE. BUT I WALKED AWAY WITH A REAL SENSE OF WHAT IT TRULY MEANS TO LEAD.

PHOTO: ILLINOIS STATE TREASURER, 1995

HERE ARE SOME THINGS I LEARNED WHILE WORKING IN

"THE SYSTEM"

- **NOTHING IS MORE IMPORTANT THAN A PERSON'S WORD**

- **DON'T PROMISE WHAT CAN'T BE DELIVERED**

- **TALK SOME, BUT LISTEN MORE**

- **SHOW UP FOR EVERYTHING**

- **BE HEARD, BUT DON'T BE A PROBLEM**

- **ALONG WITH EVERYTHING ELSE, HELP RAISE MONEY - NOBODY CAN STAY IN POLITICS WITHOUT IT**

BUT THE BIGGEST LESSON I LEARNED WAS
TO TAKE NOTHING FOR GRANTED

After months of preparation, trips to Springfield, Illinois and Washington, D.C. and endless meetings with a group of hand-selected advisors, I decided to run for my home town seat in the Illinois State House of Representatives. Susan Deutchler was retiring after 2 years and I wanted to be the first to announce my candidacy. At Northwestern University, I'd once done a research paper on John F. Kennedy. I recalled a speech he'd given in downtown Aurora on September 24, 1963. Thirty-seven years later I gave my own announcement, a little Camelot flair by kicking off my campaign on the same date in the same place.

Beri Eljera, in the Asian Week Magazine wrote: Making History in Illinois

He went to college to become a doctor, just like his father. But an audacious - and successful - candidacy as student body president of Valparaiso University in Indiana changed his life forever. Now, Ravi Singh, who admits he is hopelessly hooked on politics, wants to take his political ambition further: he wants to be the first Asian Pacific American elected to the Illinois Legislature.

Mark Foster, in the Kane County Chronicle wrote: Asian American ask religious and age issues.

a 25-year old Sikh who grew up in Aurora and became an aide in state government, stood about 100 feet from the site used by Kennedy and asked voters to overlook his age and religion in his Republican primary bid for the 42nd District seat in the Illinois House of Representatives.

Hal Dardick, in the Chicago Tribune wrote:
GOP House hopeful launches campaign with not to Camelot.

SINGH: *"If I give up my identity and values, I'll not be an Asian. I'll not even be an American. I'm a nobody."*

Singh said he has been advised by some people that he should take off his Turban and shave off his beard. "I am challenging the hat." Singh said, "You have to be proud of your identity."

Robert L. Kaiser, in the Chicago Tribune
wrote: Following their dreams

Alone in his car in rush-hour traffic, Ravi Singh begins to mumble. For almost 20 minutes, words spill softly from his lips as he says his morning prayers. Here, on a ramp at the Eisenhower Expressway interchange with Interstate Highway 88, his Indian faith merges with the American dream. Turban on his head and tie cinched around his neck, Singh - a state government worker and aspiring statehouse candidate - is a composite of the city's Indian community: unobtrusively holding to a few old customs while easing into the American mainstream - and the road to political power.

Eric Krol, in the Daily Herald wrote: Political Novice already old hand at raising money

With less than two weeks to go until the March 17 primary, political rookie Ravi Singh has raised more than twice the money of his closest competitor in his quest to become state legislator.

On the campaign trail, I took part in a parade celebrating the 50th anniversary of India's independence. Walking through downtown Chicago, I heard one of the parade attendees screaming, "Ravi Singh Zindabad!" Surprised, I smiled and gave the crowd my best political wave." Meanwhile, I leaned over and asked an Indian movie star walking next to me, "What did he just say?" The movie star translated, "Long live Ravi Singh." Stunned by such strong sentiments, a thousand thoughts filled my mind. What was I doing? What had I started? Was I really running for office with a turban in the United States of America?

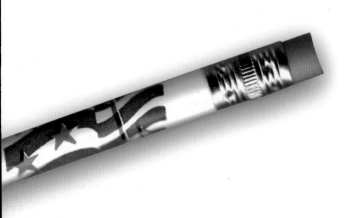

Before I ran I knew I'd have to deal with the "good ol' boys" system that permeated Illinois politics. I hoped to get their blessings. Failing that, I hoped to convince them not to work against me. And if they were determined to stand in my way, at the very least, I hoped to make them understand why I wore a turban. This, in itself, was a major campaign. With the help of my good friend and public relations specialist, Monica Collins, she arranged meetings with groups of local and state politicians and top Illinois political consultant Jim Thacker. We called it our hit list. At meeting after meeting, I stated my case to the "good ol' boys." Most of them gave it to me straight. They felt I would have to remove my turban in order to win. Some of them even told me, "You don't have a chance in hell of winning!" Their comments were discouraging, but I believed in what I was doing. Finally, Tom Coughlin, the mayor of Geneva, stood up for me and said, "You have the fire in your belly." His support soon led to endorsements from others.

In order to win, I knew I'd have to work every room I entered. From the time I walked in the door, to the time I reached the other side, I made sure everyone knew the guy with the turban. People started referring to me as "Ravi Singh the politician." Even at Sikh *Gurudwara's* - our house of worship - it became a common introduction. There are a lot of Ravi Singhs in the world. That's because Ravi is a very common first name. And the surname Singh is given to Sikhs for religious reasons - to circumvent the notorious caste system. So, from California to New York, I was now known as "Ravi Singh, politician vala" or "Ravi Singh, who is running for politics."

PHOTO: JESSE PISENO CAMPAIGN YARDSIGN

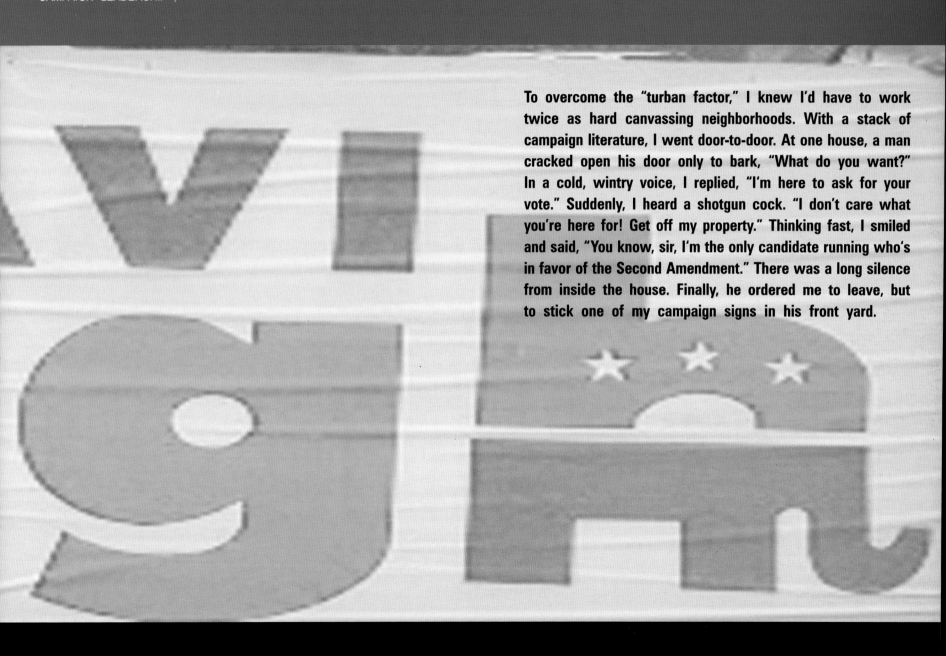

To overcome the "turban factor," I knew I'd have to work twice as hard canvassing neighborhoods. With a stack of campaign literature, I went door-to-door. At one house, a man cracked open his door only to bark, "What do you want?" In a cold, wintry voice, I replied, "I'm here to ask for your vote." Suddenly, I heard a shotgun cock. "I don't care what you're here for! Get off my property." Thinking fast, I smiled and said, "You know, sir, I'm the only candidate running who's in favor of the Second Amendment." There was a long silence from inside the house. Finally, he ordered me to leave, but to stick one of my campaign signs in his front yard.

PHOTO: 4TH OF JULY PARADE & POURING COFFEE @ MR. AJAZI GENEVA DINNER

To prove my willingness to serve, I decided to travel from diner to diner in my district, pouring coffee for thirsty customers. With an apron tied around my neck, my plan was to treat supporters and non-supporters alike to a cup of joe. *"Seva"* in Sikhism, means "selfless service." And I figured if I was going to be a public servant, this was the best way for me to start serving.

Even though the responses from people was terrific, I lost my first bid for public office in the primary on March 17. To date, no Sikh American has successfully won a state or national public office with a turban.

I WAS GOING TO ASK PEOPLE FOR THEIR VOTE, I FIGURED I SHOULD BE WILLING TO SERVE. AND IF THAT MEANT SERVING THEM COFFEE TO EARN THEIR VOTE, SO BE IT. YOU DON'T HAVE TO BE FLASHY. YOU JUST NEED TO BE SINCERE. AND IT CAN ALL START WITH A "CUP OF JOE."

PHOTO: MARTIN L. KING BIRTHDAY, YOUTH LEADERSHIP CONFERENCE.

I was representing everyone. I knew all along that my campaign was going to be an uphill battle. Little did I realize, that was just the beginning! Even though I lost that election, I continue to rely on the skills I learned. Today, I find myself campaigning every day of my life. Just to wear my turban. And to help people understand it.

In campaign leadership you need acceptance, a message, and a lot of money. In fact, any Asian American who runs for public office should expect to raise over twice the amount of money they'd otherwise need. And it was no different for me. My advisors did what they could to help me. (Although even they wished I could look just a little bit more "American.") Monica, in particular, was fantastic. Being introduced by a tall red-headed Irish woman gave me instant legitimacy. It made my campaign more universal. It was pretty clear that I wasn't just representing guys with turbans.

IF YOU ARE A SON, BE A GOOD SON.
IF YOU ARE A DAUGHTER, BE A GOOD DAUGHTER.
IF YOU ARE A BROTHER, BE A GOOD BROTHER.
IF YOU ARE A SISTER, BE A GOOD SISTER.
IF YOUR A HUSBAND, BE A GOOD HUSBAND.
IF YOU ARE A WIFE, BE A GOOD WIFE.

WHO EVER YOU ARE
BE YOUR "RELATIONSHIP."

IF YOU DON'T, YOU DO INJUSTICE TO THE TITLE.

In 1969, my parents moved to America. It was a typical immigrant's story. My father studied to become a doctor. My mother, a new bride just 20 years old, had never traveled anywhere in her life. Together, they came to believe in the American dream, living day by day in hopes of providing a better life for my younger brother, Simer, and my sister, Savina.

We all come from somewhere. I was born in Illinois. My mother was born in India. My father was born in Burma. And his parents came from what is now Pakistan. Knowing our family heritage can play an important part in developing our leadership skills. By investigating the past, we can learn from the examples set by our ancestors.

My family is a crucial part of my life. They're the ones who brought me into this world. And for that, I give them my respect and my acceptance. Respect and acceptance are the most important elements of family leadership. I may not agree with my family all the time, but I respect their wisdom. Only by accepting that there isn't another person in the world who can be our biological father, mother, brother, sister, uncle, aunt or grandparent, can one begin to learn from these relationships. It's up to us to uncover stories, up to us to nurture that love. Families may test us, but they also prepare us for life. The hardships, the laughter and the memories allow us to develop a compassionate side to our

leadership qualities.

PHOTO: SIKH MARRIAGE CLIPART DESIGNED BY WEARETHESOLUTION.COM

FAMILY LIFE IS NO FAIRY TALE.

Arranged marriages are not a part of the Sikh religion. But they've become a part of our culture as Indian parents place a subtle, silent pressure on their children to marry within the faith. This silence grows to a loud roar when you add pressure from the community. Maybe that's why the divorce rate in India is in the single digits. Because their culture believes real love can only blossom over time. But the children of Indian immigrants have expectations based on their American culture, too. Every Sikh dreams of finding happiness - the perfect balance between two people and two cultures. And they hope to do it without making their parents too mad at them in the process. No relationship is easy. Throw in two cultures and things get even more difficult. I sometimes think our chances of finding the right person are about as good as our chances of winning the lottery. But that's exactly what a successful relationship feels like, too.

YOU HAVE TO LEARN TO BALANCE BOTH YOUR WORLDS.

People have trouble understanding that you can wear a turban, have brown skin, and still be an American. When I was 16 years old, I began filling out college applications. So I asked my parents what I was. They gave me a strange look. I explained that I needed to mark down what I was on the application, but I couldn't find a box for me. I wasn't an African-American or a Native American and the box for Asians was intended for Chinese, Japanese or Koreans. There was just one option left. I had to mark myself down as an "other."

DISCOVERING YOUR ROOTS IS THE KEY TO HALF YOUR IDENTITY. THE REST IS UP TO YOU.

Growing up as an "other" is difficult. Dating, in particular, was a constant challenge. Some women found my turban intimidating. Others thought of it as something mystical. My social life has always been a delicate balance between America and India, between right and wrong, and between religion and culture. I believe each culture has its good points. For example, Sikhism prides itself on being one of the first religions in the world to grant equality to women. Unmarried women were even given a separate last name. Kaur, which means "princess," to circumvent the caste system. But American culture has much to offer, as well. Americans like to talk about their relationships. Indians do not. I often wondered if it was even possible to balance the two worlds. But I was reassured by the words of my childhood friend Brian Goodger, who once told me, "I know growing up in America with a turban can be rough but as long as we have friendship it can't be that bad."

I FOUND OUT I WAS AN "OTHER"

PHOTO: SAVINA KAUR SINGH WITH OLDER BROTHER.

On a business trip to San Diego, I was enjoying the perfect weather on a walk downtown. I passed a pair of college students, banging out in the street near a group of homeless people. Once they were out of eye contact. I heard one of them yell at me, "Hey, Bennie!" I automatically checked my watch.

PHOTO: NEW YORK TWIN TOWERS 09-11-01

It had been months since September 11. Were people going to be calling me for Osama Bin Laden for the rest of my life? I suppose I could have kept walking. But this time, I turned around and walked back to this odd group of college kids and homeless people. I'll admit, I was partially motivated by curiosity. Who had yelled at me? The young and the educated? Or society's old and discarded? To my surprise, one of the college kids freely admitted to it. I didn't know what to say. But my homeless friends did. "That was really rude," one of them scolded the students. I laughed to myself. Only in America could an educated person be less enlightened than a person who lives in the streets.

In the aftermath of September 11, 2001 the meaning of community has taken on new significance. We're even more proud to be Americans and we're even more willing to lend each other a hand. But for me, the weeks following 9/11 also brought the hatred, bigotry and ignorance of some Americans to the forefront. I talked to Sikh mothers who said in the aftermath of September 11, 2001 the meaning of community has taken on new significance. We're even their children were being harassed. Other Sikhs complained that they weren't being allowed to enter buildings downtown. Our community scrambled to come up with a plan of action. We considered placing an advertisement in the local newspaper. But how much good could one advertisement do in the face of so much ignorance?

I was never more aware of how my turban looked to other people than in the days following 9/11. At the grocery store, a person walked up to me and said, "We forgive you. We know it's not your fault." At a rally held at City Hall in Chicago, people told me, "God bless you" and "God forgive you." All I could do was smile. Although I wear a turban, the fact is, Sikhs share nothing religiously, politically or geographically with people of the Muslim faith.

PHOTO: WINTER STATE CAPITOL SPRINGFIELD, ILLINOIS

I knew I couldn't educate everyone I met about the fifth largest religion in the world. Not in the 15 seconds or so we shared. But it never occurred to me to take offence at the ignorance of my fellow Americans, either. It was better than avoiding them altogether.

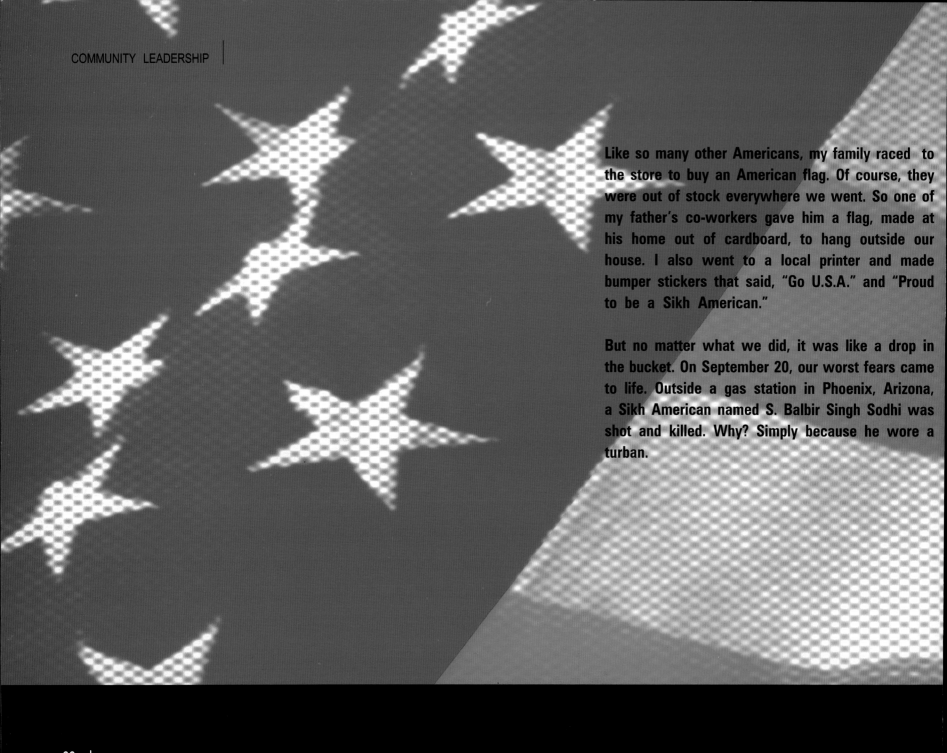

Like so many other Americans, my family raced to the store to buy an American flag. Of course, they were out of stock everywhere we went. So one of my father's co-workers gave him a flag, made at his home out of cardboard, to hang outside our house. I also went to a local printer and made bumper stickers that said, "Go U.S.A." and "Proud to be a Sikh American."

But no matter what we did, it was like a drop in the bucket. On September 20, our worst fears came to life. Outside a gas station in Phoenix, Arizona, a Sikh American named S. Balbir Singh Sodhi was shot and killed. Why? Simply because he wore a turban.

After this stunning event, we gave up on the idea of placing an advertisement. Instead, we contacted police officers, airplane pilots and local public servants ourselves. No newspaper was going to educate our fellow Americans. It was up to us. It was up to our community. In the face of so much tragedy, it was an important lesson I needed to learn. We all have to do our part.

In post 9/11 America, many things have finally gone back to normal. But traveling with a turban has not. The airlines assure us their policy of selecting passengers for more thorough security checks is entirely random. Which must mean it's just an amazing coincidence that the guy with the turban (me) is singled out every single time he tries to board an airplane. Most of the time, airline personnel are friendly about it. But some of the smaller carriers rely on their overworked flight attendants to do the job. This can lead to some rather impatient confrontations. Like the attendant who put her face within two inches of mine and demanded I remove my turban.

I wondered if this was really necessary, until she summoned airport security and convinced me otherwise. "Is there a problem here?" The security guard asked me. Not unless you consider racial profiling a problem. I popped off my turban and showed them what the metal detector had already told them. The only thing under my turban was my head. But there is hope at the end of this story. Once the "random" search was over, I gathered my things and glanced up at the passengers waiting behind me. Most of them actually looked sorry for me. Maybe things are going back to normal after all.

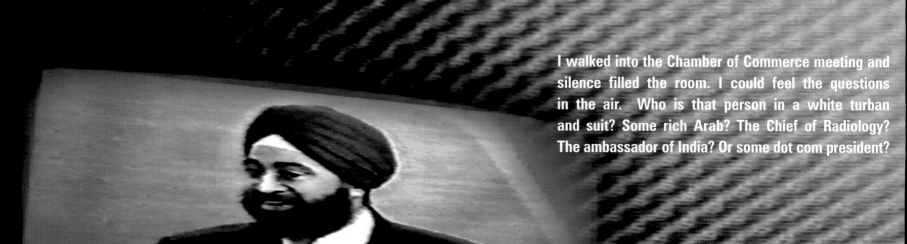

I walked into the Chamber of Commerce meeting and silence filled the room. I could feel the questions in the air. Who is that person in a white turban and suit? Some rich Arab? The Chief of Radiology? The ambassador of India? Or some dot com president?

PHOTO: INTERVIEW CNBC ON ELECTIONMALL.COM

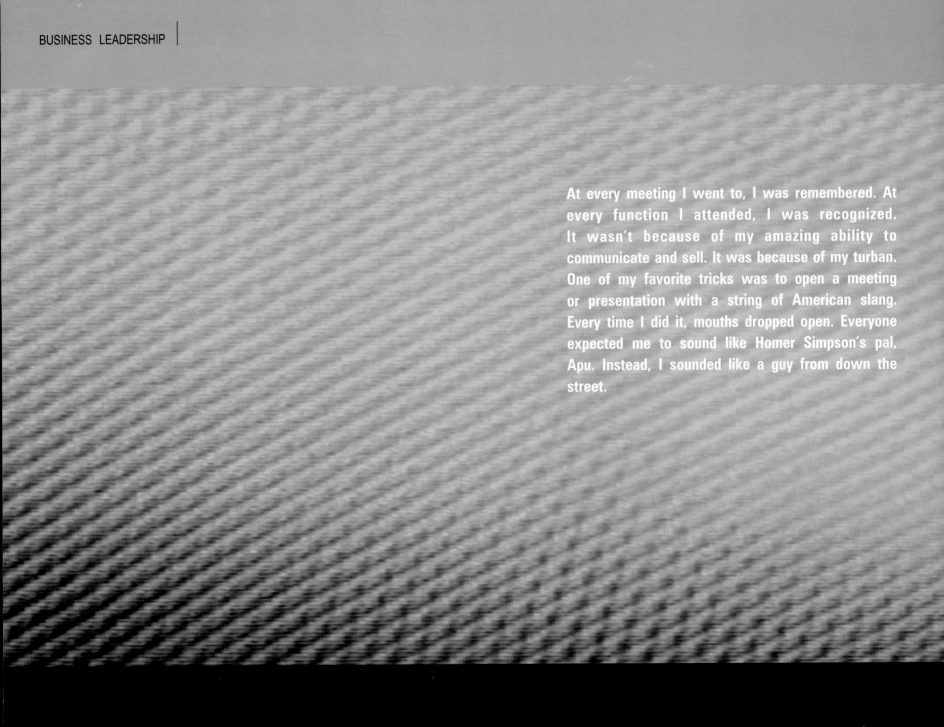

At every meeting I went to, I was remembered. At every function I attended, I was recognized. It wasn't because of my amazing ability to communicate and sell. It was because of my turban. One of my favorite tricks was to open a meeting or presentation with a string of American slang. Every time I did it, mouths dropped open. Everyone expected me to sound like Homer Simpson's pal, Apu. Instead, I sounded like a guy from down the street.

Sometimes, I wonder if I started my own business because it was easier than getting hired with a turban. Whatever the reason, when the dot com boom hit like a tidal wave, I decided to get my feet wet. My first thought was to start selling turbans on the Internet - since you can't really find them at the local shopping mall. Instead, I started a small Internet advertising marketing company called WeAreTheSolution.com Inc.™

SOMETIMES YOU MUST PICTURE
WHAT YOU SEE YOURSELF BECOMING
IN ORDER TO BECOME WHAT YOU MUST

This forced me to draw on all the leadership skills I'd ever learned, from every facet of my life. And when I didn't know something, I learned it as quickly as possible. Later, I launched www.electionmall.com, which provided e-campaigning services. By September 2000, the Republican National Committee was a client and we were sending out emails for George W. Bush.

ElectionMall Technologies Inc.

But when it comes to leadership skills in business, I learned a lot more from listening than I ever did from talking. Before I could lead, I had to learn how to follow others - every day of my life. In every workplace, environment and situation, you'll find people who've been around longer than we have. They can teach us more in one day than we'd be able to learn in a year on our own. Leadership is not about bossing people around. It's about teamwork. No matter what they're buying, selling or building, every company has a common goal. To succeed. And together, a team can achieve more than an individual.

LISTEN AND LISTEN OFTEN WISDOM COMES FROM AGE AND IT COST NOTHING BUT PAYS BIG.

PHOTO: LISTENING TO ILLINOIS GOVERNOR GEORGE RYAN

I AM A SINGH, WHICH MEANS LION.

SO IN BUSINESS I ACT LIKE ONE.

In business, there are no limits. We just need to picture ourselves as a success. If we have a vision - a vision of ourselves in the future - we'll eventually make it. As for me, I'm still working towards that goal. At one time, during the heyday of the dot com boom, my businesses were valued in the millions. Now, they're in the thousands. But that's OK. It's easy to quit when things aren't going our way. It takes discipline to stay and pick up the pieces. There's nothing wrong with making mistakes. Every obstacle has a solution.

PHOTO: WEARETHESOLUTION.COM INC BUSINESS MEETING

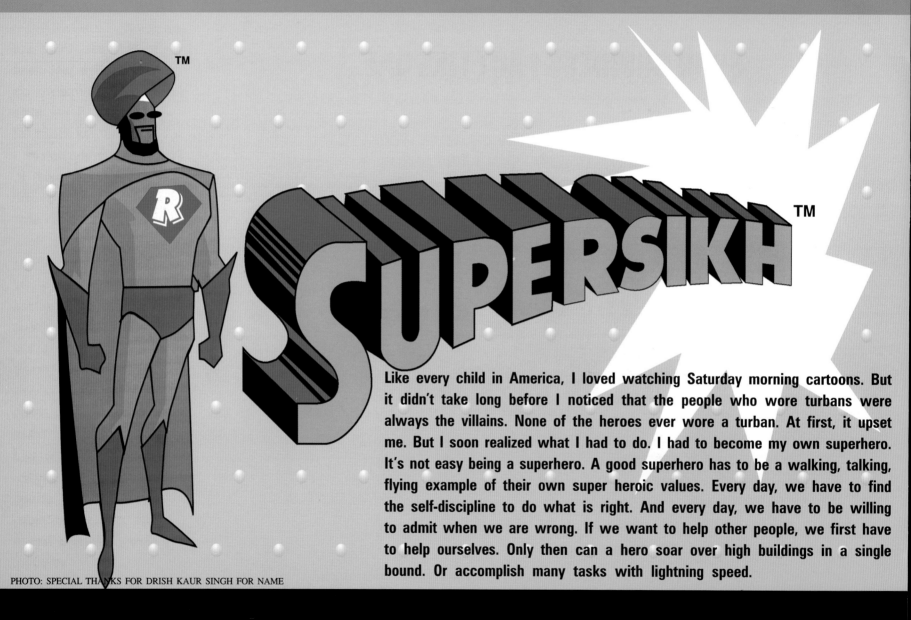

SUPERSIKH ™

Like every child in America, I loved watching Saturday morning cartoons. But it didn't take long before I noticed that the people who wore turbans were always the villains. None of the heroes ever wore a turban. At first, it upset me. But I soon realized what I had to do. I had to become my own superhero. It's not easy being a superhero. A good superhero has to be a walking, talking, flying example of their own super heroic values. Every day, we have to find the self-discipline to do what is right. And every day, we have to be willing to admit when we are wrong. If we want to help other people, we first have to help ourselves. Only then can a hero soar over high buildings in a single bound. Or accomplish many tasks with lightning speed.

PHOTO: SPECIAL THANKS FOR DRISH KAUR SINGH FOR NAME

People say, "Keep your friends close, but keep your enemies closer." That's wise advice. Because we can always count on our enemies to point out our flaws. People who care about us tend to overlook our faults. Leaders can grow by discovering their strengths and working to improve those.

But we can also grow by discovering our weaknesses and working to correct those. Of course, not all faults can be fixed. Superman is weakened by Kryptonite. So he avoids it. He finds a way to go around it. I'm disorganized. That's my Achilles' heel. But I've found ways to compensate for it. I count on other people to help me get organized. It can be quite a challenge. But it's worth it.

Because I am my own superhero, I wear my turban with confidence. Every day of my life. That's not an easy thing to do as a visible minority in America. I've endured my share of embarrassing moments in public. Whether it was getting beaten up by the school bully or being turned down for a job. Life is full of challenges. But I meet them with a simple formula that reminds me how to deal with things on four levels: physically, intellectually, emotionally and spiritually. (Or "P.I.E.S." for short.) Physically, I keep myself healthy. Intellectually, I educate myself constantly. Emotionally, I keep my feelings and impulses under control. And spiritually, I accept that there is a divine plan and surrender to it. I like to think of it as "keeping my P.I.E.S. in order." And it's my super secret weapon when things aren't going well.

P **I** **E** **S**

SPECIAL THANKS TO MICHAEL CLAY FOR 'PIES' CONCEPT

LIFE IS LIKE A ROLLER COASTER. THERE ARE UPS AND DOWNS. WE JUST HAVE TO LEARN HOW TO DEAL WITH THEM.

As leaders, our challenge is to avoid the deepest troughs. To keep things constant. It's little bit of Eastern philosophy mixed with something from the West. And for me, it's worked wonders.

Life comes at us in waves. Sometimes we find ourselves at the crest. Other times we're down in the trough. Sikh theology has names for these two extremes - *Sukh* (happiness) at the top and *Dukh* (sadness) at the bottom. We don't think much about keeping our P.I.E.S. in order at the top of the wave.

But we should. By maintaining ourselves physically, intellectually, emotionally and spiritually at *Sukh*, we'll have an easier time when *Dukh* happens. In fact, *Dukh* will feel more like a ripple than a tidal wave. And the bad moments won't seem so overwhelming.

WE ALL HAVE OUR FANTASIES

WE MUST NEVER STOP BELIEVING

THE ONLY BARRIERS ARE THE ONES WE CREATE

PHOTO: TURBAN 007

SINGH 007

Whenever I see another person with a turban, I get excited. In America, you just don't see a lot people wearing turbans. When I do, I can't help liking them instantly. Because we're both going through the same stuff every day, I feel like I already know them. I call this phenomenon "turban branding." There are actually a lot of benefits to being branded by my turban. For example, people often ask me if I know so-and-so - a person they know with a turban who happens to be a nice guy. I almost always don't but it's nice to be associated with good people just because of my turban. Unfortunately, it works the other way, too. When someone like Ayatollah Khomeini or Osama Bin Laden makes the news, people assume I must be "one of them." At times like that, wearing a turban can be a pretty costly brand.

Anyone who wears a turban can relate to the funny, hurtful, sad, curious, ignorant, rude and often downright bizarre assumptions other people make about them. At the every least, this "turban talk" makes for some pretty amusing stories. . .

During an interview at the state capitol, I was asked if my turban would get in the way. I said, "No, not really. The ceilings in the capitol are pretty high."

In school, the student sitting behind me complained that he couldn't see over my turban. So the teacher seated me in the back of the class.

At a convenience store, a young boy pointed at me and shouted, "Look, Mommy! A genie!"

"What does the color of your turban mean?" Someone asked me. I replied, "My canny ability to match my clothes!"

Someone once asked me, "Where do you come from?" I said, "From Chicago." They said, "No, where do you really come from?" So I said, "From my mother. Why?"

One day in grade school, I forgot to bring anything for "Show and Tell." So I taught the class how to tie a turban.

"What's under your turban?" someone asked me. I replied, "My hair!" and popped it right off to show him.

I've always been interested in seeing people reach their full potential. I believe most of us just need a little push. Today's market-driven society treats us like dummies looking for easy answers and quick solutions. It teaches us that success can only be defined by the number of material possessions we accumulate. But that's the easy way out. And people who are given the easy way out won't have the tools they need to achieve their long-term desires. The sum of all my experiences - from being the first turban-wearing cadet in an American military academy to running for public office with a turban to starting my own companies - have been more valuable to me than anything I could ever buy. Material wealth is not the answer. It's who you are - and what you do - that is priceless. In many ways, we are all wearing our own turbans. I hope that you have gained some insight into what it means to wear a turban in America today. And

Lead yourself. Push the norm. Go beyond. Every step is a step in your direction. No matter if you have a turban or not. We all wear our own turbans that help us define who we are. I have to admit, My turban is my biggest asset. I am who I am because of my turban.

An Internet pioneer, Ravi Singh was politically savvy at an early age. At 25, Ravi's passion for politics became obvious when he ran for public office for the Illinois General Assembly. During his campaign, he made history by launching the first "online chat - town hall meeting" and became the first Asian Indian American to run for the Illinois State House of Representatives.

In 1995, Ravi taught citizens at the Illinois State Fair "how to use the Internet and surf Yahoo!™." Prior to his run for public office, Ravi worked as an administrative assistant for the Illinois Lt. Governor and State Treasurer. In 1997, he was promoted to Director of Community Relations for the State Treasurer. During this time, he was asked to serve on Bob Dole's National Asian American Planning Committee collecting "Internet email addresses" for the 1996 Presidential Election.

In 1999, Ravi founded a private start-up, technology-advertising company, @wearethesolution.com. In 2000, he filed for international patents related to online fundraising and political emails, eYardsigns™ under ElectionMall.com, also known as Election Mall Technologies (EMT). EMT is a non-partisan company that offers campaign technology services via the World Wide Web. EMT has advised and assisted several campaigns including the 2000 presidential campaign for George W. Bush and has sent emails for members of the Democratic National Committee. EMT won the prestigious "Pollie Award" for technology in 2002 from the American Association of Political Consultants (AAPC) with strategic partner Chicago Kent College of Law for the online project "electionelaw.com."

Ravi graduated as a United States 2nd Lieutenant from Marmion Military Academy and has a Bachelors of Science from Valparaiso University. He has a Masters degree in Political Science from Northwestern University and a Masters degree in Executive Business Administration from Loyola Marymount University.

Ravi has lectured on online politics and been a guest on MSNBC™ "Power Lunch Asia." Recently he was featured in an article for USA Weekend magazine in which he was named one of the "five new powerbrokers whose sites and bytes may well influence how you cast your ballot come November." Ravi is a founder and non-partisan director of the Midwest Chapter Board of Directors of the AAPC. Ravi Singh is currently the CEO of Election Mall Technologies.

Websites on Sikh Religion

www.sikhnet.com	www.sikhs.org	www.khalsapride.com	www.sikhmedia.org
www.sikhnet.com/HemkuntSahib/	www.sikhvideos.org	www.sikhitothemax.com	www.sikhpoint.com
www.sikhseek.com	www.sikhmuseum.org	www.spiritborn.org	www.sikhsfortechnology.com
www.sikh.net	www.sikhspirit.com	www.unitedsikhs.org	www.sikhprofessionals.org
www.allaboutsikhs.com	www.sikhfoundation.org	www.sikhtoons.com	www.srigurugranthsahib.org
www.sikh-history.com	www.sgpc.net	www.sikhheritage.org	www.punjabiamericanheritagesociety.org
			www.sikh-religion.de (in Deutsch)

Legal Disclaimer : These internet web links are not an endorsement of any kind and are to be used as a reference only.